# PHILIP
## OF
# TEXAS

## JAMES OTIS

**NOTGRASS**
HISTORY

Cover painting by Edward Mitchell Bannister, 1877
Smithsonian American Art Museum, Gift of Louis Glaser

**NOTGRASS
HISTORY**

Gainesboro, Tennessee
notgrass.com

Originally published in 1913 by the American Book Company
This edition © 2020 by Notgrass History

Cover design by Mary Evelyn McCurdy
Interior design by Jonathan Lewis (JonlinCreative.com)

ISBN 978-1-60999-148-7
Printed and Bound in the United States of America

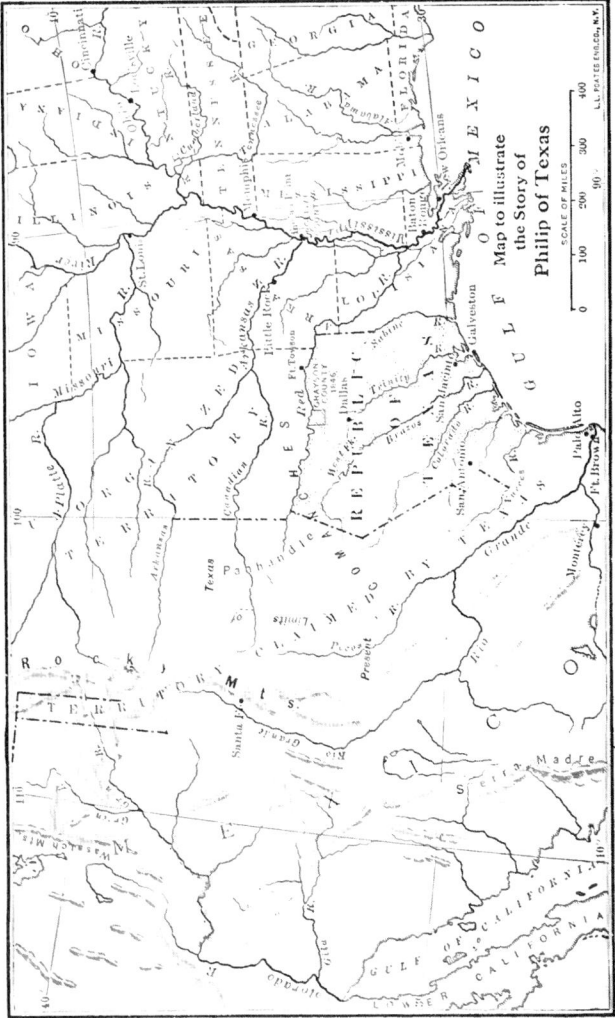

Map to illustrate
the Story of
**Philip of Texas**

SCALE OF MILES

0    100    200    300    400

L.L. POATES ENG. CO., N.Y.

# CONTENTS

## CHAPTER NINE

## CHAPTER TEN

## CHAPTER ELEVEN

## CHAPTER TWELVE

## CHAPTER THIRTEEN

## CHAPTER FOURTEEN

## CHAPTER FIFTEEN

## CHAPTER SIXTEEN

# EDITOR'S NOTE

In preparing this edition of *Philip of Texas*, I have omitted certain passages related to animals that contain gory detail. I have also omitted a few passages that I felt would be tedious for today's young readers. Most of the story, however, remains in its original form.

At the time this story takes place, many people of European descent treated native and enslaved people unjustly through their words and actions. The original version of *Philip of Texas* contains some offensive comments about these people. For this edition I have altered or omitted those comments. The story still has enslaved characters and speaks of conflict between "Indians" and people of European descent.

Learning about these aspects of American history is important, but learning about them is not the same as condoning them. They were a part of real life for many people in our country. We must learn about our nation's past—both good and bad—so that we are better equipped to make America a better place today.

*Mary Evelyn McCurdy, Editor*

# CHAPTER
# ONE

---

## MY DREAMS OF A SHEEP RANCH

The day I was twelve years old, Father gave me twelve ewes out of his flock of seventy-two, counting these sheep as payment for the work I had done in tending them. Even at that time I thought myself a good shepherd, for I was able to keep a small flock well together.

With Gyp, our dog, I could have herded five hundred as readily as I did seventy-two, because on our plantation in Mississippi the pastures were fenced. Therefore when Father began to talk of moving to Texas and there making a venture in the cattle business, I decided at once that if he did so, it should be

my aim to raise sheep. With this idea I gathered from the neighbors roundabout, who had larger flocks than ours, all the possible information about the business in our own state.

# SHEEP RAISING

A sheep will yield about five pounds of wool each year, and you can count that each animal in a herd will give you one dollar's worth of its fleece annually. Of course there is considerable expense, if one is obliged to pay for shearing, or for dipping, in case that disease known as "scab" comes among the flock.

It is pretty certain that during the year there will be as many lambs born as there are sheep in the flock, and if a sheep is worth five dollars, you can reckon the lamb at three, for it will be a yearling in twelve months, and a full-grown sheep a year later. So one can say that every sheep worth five dollars will bring in a profit of four dollars each year, less the expense of keeping.

Think of the profit of five hundred sheep in one year! Suppose they cost you for herding, shearing, and dipping, in case you cannot manage the flock yourself, three hundred dollars. You get two thousand dollars for the wool and the increase in the flock, and pay out three hundred. This leaves seventeen hundred dollars clear profit in one year from five hundred sheep, and that is not a large flock.

Now it might seem as if this matter of raising sheep, and the profit to be had from them, could have no influence in deciding my going from the state of Mississippi to the Republic of Texas, and yet if it had not been for my hope of one day owning a big sheep ranch, I would not have been so delighted when Father began to talk of making a new home in that country which had so lately separated from Mexico.

## SOMETHING ABOUT TEXAS

One might suppose that my father was a shiftless sort of man to make a change of homes after he had a boy twelve years old; but that is not the fact, as you will understand when I tell you why we sold the plantation in Mississippi, where we were raising fairly good crops of cotton, to embark in the cattle business in Texas.

Of course, it is not necessary for me to relate that the people in Texas declared themselves independent of Mexico in the year 1836, as in 1776 the colonists determined to be free men in a free country, and so broke away from England and England's king.

No doubt you already know that it was on the twenty-second day of April in the year 1836, the day after the battle of San Jacinto, that General Houston captured the Mexican general, Santa Anna; a treaty was then made between Texas and Mexico, which allowed the Texans to become an independent nation. You are also acquainted with the troubles in Texas, when, in the year 1840, the Comanches overran the country, and you have heard of the capture of the town of San Antonio by the Mexicans in September of the year 1842.

# LAND GRANTS

All this has little to do with what I am going to tell in regard to my going into the sheep business; yet if all those things had not happened, then President Lamar and President Houston might not have been able to make grants of land to people who were willing to come into the country and build homes.

There were a number of men who succeeded in getting so-called grants from the Texan government. Among these there was a certain Mr. Peters,—I never knew his first name,—who had obtained a grant of an exceedingly large tract of land in the northern part. It was, so Father had been told, the best land in Texas; and in order to gain settlers, Mr. Peters agreed to give outright to the head of every family six hundred and forty acres of land, and to each single man three hundred and twenty acres.

Now, of course, my father was the head of a family, although Mother and I were the only other members of it; nevertheless he would receive just as many acres of land as though he had a dozen children.

When the matter was first talked about among our neighbors in Mississippi, I hoped I might be counted as a single man; but I was very soon made to understand that a lad of twelve years was mistaken when he reckoned himself of sufficient age to have given him three hundred and twenty acres of land simply for going into a country and living there.

# THE "TEXAS FEVER"

Because of this offer by Mr. Peters, the people around us, whose plantations were not particularly valuable, were highly excited, for all had heard how rich was the land in the Republic of Texas, and how well it was adapted for cattle raising.

While Mother and Father were talking the matter over, trying to decide whether they would go into Peters's colony, I heard him tell her that already a great many people from Missouri, Illinois, Indiana, and Kentucky, as well as from our state, had gone there and had sent back the most cheering words regarding the possibility of making money in that new country.

Perhaps I should say that this grant was made to the Peters colony early in the year 1842, but it was not until the spring of the next year that Father began to have what some of our neighbors laughingly called the "Texas Fever"; and I took it because of the possibilities of raising sheep.

It was just about this time that the Texans began to talk of being annexed to the United States, for their republic was not so flourishing as many would have liked to see it. The country was in debt to the amount of nearly seven million dollars, so I heard Father say, and the people stood in fear of the Mexicans on the one side, who were ever ready to make trouble, and of the Indians on the other, to say nothing of the wild beasts everywhere.

Such a thinly settled country could not raise large armies to fight off their enemies, and those people who had been living for some time in Texas believed that if their republic could become a part of the United States, they would have all the soldiers that were needed to keep peace in the land.

# WHY I WANTED TO GO INTO TEXAS

Of all this I knew very little at the time Father was talking about making a new home, and I cared less, for my mind was filled entirely with the idea of one day owning a large sheep ranch. From the time I began to take care of Father's flock I had heard people, lately come from Texas, declare that that was the one spot in all the wide world where sheep could be raised easily and at small cost.

There were other reasons besides this which caused me to hope that my father would decide to make a change of homes. I had heard that the ponies, which the Texans called mustangs, could be bought for from eight to twenty dollars each, and that they cost no more to keep than ordinary cows, for they did not require grain. Now, in all my life, I had never owned either horse or pony, for the only driving animals on our Mississippi plantation had been mules.

# CHAPTER
# TWO

___

## HUNTING IN TEXAS

I had also read that there was much good hunting in Texas, and that one need not go very far afield in order to find plenty of bears; in fact, that there were too many for the comfort of the sheep raisers. I knew also that deer were to be found in large numbers and that there were cougars, which are called Mexican lions, and panthers, together with wildcats and wolves. Fancy such a list of game as that for a fellow who was as fond of shooting as I was!

Then again, one of our neighbors who had been in Texas told me of the wild hogs, or peccaries, as they are sometimes called, that go in droves of from half

a dozen to twenty or thirty, and are very fierce when stirred up.

The wolves concerned me most just then, for you know that these animals are exceedingly fond of sheep, and he who herds a flock on the range must keep his eyes wide open for those four-footed enemies. Three kinds of wolves were to be found in Texas: the black wolf which was rare, the coyote, and the lobo or gray wolf. The last two were great sheep stealers and many in number.

It seemed to me then, as it has many times since, that it would be great sport to hunt those sheep eaters and lay up a goodly stock of their pelts, for a wolf hide, when taken in the proper season, makes an excellent bed covering, whether it be in a house or on the open prairie.

From the time that Father began to talk of joining Peters's colony, I spent a good portion of my time learning all that was possible concerning this republic, the people of which were eager to come into the

United States. I found, as any one can who will make diligent search, the most interesting stories not only about hunting, but about the early troubles between Texas and Mexico, the Texans' fight for independence, and the many Indian raids.

## FATHER GOES TO SPY OUT THE LAND

It seemed to me that Father and Mother spent a great deal of unnecessary time in discussing whether they would change their home from Mississippi to Texas. In fact I was beginning to despair of ever becoming a sheep raiser in the Peters colony, when Father suddenly declared that he would go to see the country for himself, and if it was half as good as people said it was, he would lay out his claim of six hundred and forty acres and come back to sell the plantation and move the livestock.

I begged hard to be allowed to go with him, but my request was not to be granted, for although we owned two slaves, John and Zeba, I must be the one to look after the cattle, the sheep, and the mules.

Therefore it was decided that I should be the head of the family while Father was away, and so proud was I over being given such a position of trust, that

I failed to grieve, as I otherwise might have done, at not being allowed to go with him.

He set out with a pair of our best mules hitched to a light wagon, intending to drive to Little Rock in Arkansas, and from there to Fort Towson, after which he would make his way across what is now Grayson County, spying out the land.

# OUR PLANTATION IN MISSISSIPPI

It was not a very long journey, although he would probably travel two or three hundred miles before turning back. We lived in Bolivar County, in Mississippi, near Indian Point, where, as you know, the Arkansas River joins with the Mississippi.

Our plantation was not well suited to cotton raising, and perhaps for this reason Father was all the more willing to listen to those people who had so much to say about Texas, that one could almost believe it to be a veritable Promised Land. Father had set out to raise cattle, although our plantation was no better adapted for such a purpose, perhaps, than it was for cotton raising. We had about seventy head of oxen, and twenty mules, together with the seventy-two sheep which made up my own and my father's flocks. I did not realize that the profits from sheep raising in Texas might not be the same as in Mississippi.

I counted the days while Father was away, thinking with each sunrise that I would see him again before nightfall. After he had been gone two or three weeks I was foolish enough to wander up the road now and then, hoping to meet him on his return, and be the first to hear the good news.

# FATHER COMES HOME

He had been absent nearly six weeks, and my heart had almost grown sick with waiting, when late one night, after I had gone to bed, I heard a commotion downstairs, followed by shouts for John or Zeba, and then I recognized my father's voice.

There is little need for me to say that I tumbled, rather than ran, down the stairs, so great was my eagerness to learn the result of his visit into Texas, and even before he had had time to take me in his arms I insisted on knowing whether he had staked out his claim.

In a few words he quieted my impatience by telling me we would set off for the new country as soon as the necessary arrangements could be made. So far as the details were concerned I was willing to wait, for the matter had been settled as I hoped it would be.

Later, I learned that our new home was to be on the West Fork of the Trinity River, where, so Father said, the land was better suited for cattle or sheep raising than any other he had ever seen.

As a matter of fact he was even more delighted with the prospect of going to Texas than I was, and at once Mother fell in with the plan heartily. She knew he would not have been so pleased at taking up a claim, unless it seemed certain we could better our position very greatly, for he was a home-loving man, and would not have moved from our plantation had he not felt reasonably sure of making a change for the better.

He told us that people from the United States, and even from across the sea in France, were going in great numbers to Texas, and he had no doubt but that as soon as it was made one of the states of the Union, it would prosper beyond any land of which we had ever heard.

## THE BIGNESS OF TEXAS

Then he began to tell us how large the Republic of Texas was, and before he had finished I was filled with astonishment, for, without having given any great thought to the matter, I had fancied it might, perhaps, be somewhere near the size of our state of Mississippi.

He told us that Texas was much larger than the countries of Sweden and Norway together, three times the size of Great Britain and Ireland, and nearly twice as large as France. He also said that the area of all the New England and Middle States was considerably less than that of Texas.

Imagine such an extent of territory open to new settlers! A republic nearly eight times as large as the state of New York, nine times as large as the state of Ohio, and six times as large as all New England put together!

There was no longer any surprise in my mind that the people who made up the government of Texas would be willing to give six hundred and forty acres to every man with a family who would settle there, when, within their boundaries, they had more than two hundred million acres.

# CHAPTER

# THREE

---

## WHERE WE WERE GOING

Talk of sheep raising, and giving two acres to each sheep! If, before Father went away, I had been eager to own a sheep ranch in Texas, then certainly I was nearly wild with the idea after he returned, for from his stories I began to understand that one could own thousands upon thousands, and yet find ample room to feed them all.

We were not going, so it seemed, into the best portion of the republic for sheep raising, but rather into the northern part, while the finest grazing lands were on the western side, or in that oddly shaped piece which is called the "Panhandle."

However, I was well satisfied if we could not have the best of the sheep-raising business, if only we might embark in it anywhere.

# WHAT I HOPED TO DO

I was only twelve years old, and already owned twelve ewes. Now I well knew from what I had heard sheep raisers say, that if I attended to my little flock properly, and if they met with no accident, it would be nothing marvelous if, at the end of nine years, when I should be twenty-one, my flock had increased to five thousand, or even more.

Father had hardly finished telling Mother and me of what he had seen during his journey, before we began to make preparations for moving. Surely it seemed to me we were likely to have good fortune, for within eight and forty hours after he returned, a man came up from Baton Rouge to buy our plantation, having heard that Father was suffering with the Texas fever. Within two hours after he showed his willingness to buy our land the bargain was made, a fairly large portion of the money paid over, and Mother and I knew that within twenty days we should leave the home where I was born.

# CATTLE DRIVING

Perhaps my heart grew just a bit faint when I learned that it would be necessary to drive all our cattle and sheep from Bolivar County into Texas, and that I was expected to do a large share of the work. Father thought that John, Zeba, and I should be able to keep the cattle on the road, for we were to follow the highway the entire distance, and he intended to hire three slaves from our neighbors to drive the mules which would haul all our household belongings.

There was no question in my mind but that we would get along easily with the oxen and the cows. Father decided to harness most of the mules to three wagons, so they could be handled by the hired men;

but the question of how we would be able to get the sheep along worried me much. Whoever has had charge of such animals knows well that it is not a simple task to drive them over a strange country, however quiet they may have been on feeding grounds with which they are acquainted.

But no good could come from my worrying as to how we might get into Texas. I would soon know by experience. In fact, I had little time to concern myself about anything whatsoever save the work on hand, because in order to be ready to leave the plantation within twenty days, all of us found plenty with which to occupy our hands.

It really seemed to me as if Gyp knew exactly what we were planning to do, for he walked around at my heels day after day, with his tail hanging between his legs, as though ashamed that he was about to leave the United States for a new country, where he would see a flag which bore but a single star.

# HOW WE SET OUT

There was so much bustle and confusion on the plantation during the short time left to us that I hardly remember how we made ready; but I do know that we were finally prepared for the journey, and that John and Zeba set off with the cattle twenty-four hours before Father, Mother, and I left home, in order that the creatures might become somewhat accustomed to traveling by the time we overtook them.

We had three wagons covered with heavy cloth, each drawn by six mules, and loaded with all our provisions, clothing, and such farming tools as we wanted to take with us.

The other two mules were harnessed to the wagon in which Father had made the journey to Texas, and in this Mother was to travel, Father riding with her when he was not needed elsewhere.

My mother was a good horsewoman, and the handling of two, or even four, mules would not have troubled her in the slightest. Therefore she said to me laughingly when Gyp and I had gathered the sheep into one corner of the stable yard, ready to set off just behind the mule teams, that her part of the journey would be much like a pleasure trip, while to my share must come a goodly portion of dust and toil.

Father had hired from one of the neighbors three of his best slaves, who were to drive the mule teams, and who could be trusted to come back alone from Texas as soon as their work had been finished.

So it was that we had in our party two grown white people, one boy, five slaves, and Gyp. I am counting the dog as a member of the company, for before we arrived at the West Fork of the Trinity River he showed himself to be of quite as much importance, and of even more service, than any of the men.

# A LABORIOUS JOURNEY

John and Zeba managed to get along with the cattle very well; but the drivers of the mule teams were not so skillful in handling the animals as Father had expected, and the result was that he found it necessary to take the place of one or the other nearly all the time, thus leaving Mother alone.

Sometimes I led the procession; at other times I trudged on in the rear where the dust was thickest, running first on one side of the road and then on the other, to keep the sheep from straying, and succeeded in holding them to the true course only by the aid of my dog, who had more sound common sense in that shaggy body of his than the brightest lad I have ever come across. Gyp was a willing worker, and a cheery companion at all times. He would run here and there regardless of the heat, and when the sheep were partly straightened up as they should be, come back panting, his red tongue lolling out, and looking up at me with a world of love in his big brown eyes, as if to ask why I was so solemn, or why I could not find, as he did, some sport in thus driving a flock of silly sheep to Texas.

During the journey we halted wherever night overtook us, sometimes camping in the open and finding our beds in one of the wagons, or again herding our cattle in the stable yard of a tavern.

As for food, we got it as best we could. When fortune favored us and we came upon a tavern, we had enough to satisfy our hunger, and in very many places as good as we could have had at the old home in Bolivar County. At other times we ate from the store of provisions we carried, cooking the food by the roadside, while the sheep and the cattle, too tired to stray very far after so many miles of plodding, fed eagerly on whatever grass they were lucky enough to find.

Gyp was my bedfellow, whether I slept in one of the wagons or at a tavern, and before we had crossed the Red River I found myself treating him as I would have treated a lad of my own age, and time and time again I thought to myself that he understood all I said to him.

# CHAPTER
# FOUR

———

## COMANCHE INDIANS

Before we left the old home I firmly believed we would
meet with strange adventures on our long journey, and
each morning when we set out, I driving the sheep,
with Gyp running to and fro to make certain my work
was done properly, I felt convinced that before night
came something out of the ordinary would take place.
Yet until we came near to Fort Towson I saw nothing
more strange or entertaining than I might have seen
on the banks of the Mississippi River, but when we
were within two miles or more of the fort, and the
sheep and I were leading the way, we suddenly came
upon a band of seven Comanche Indians, the first of

the tribe I had ever seen. They were all mounted, no one of them wearing more clothing than the breech-cloth around his waist, and at least two of them armed with what I believed to be serviceable rifles.

It was as if the fellows had come up out of the very ground, so suddenly did they appear. Although I could not have understood their language if any attempt had been made to open a conversation, it was plain to me that they intended to take possession of my sheep as well as of those belonging to Father, while I did not doubt but that they would make quick work of me.

# FATHER COMES TO MY RESCUE

It is more than likely that all my fears might have been realized had the remainder of our party been very far in the rear, for I believe the Indians thought I was alone on the road, driving the flock to Fort Towson where it could be slaughtered; but at the very moment when two of the most frightening of the party dismounted and came toward me with their rifles in hand, Father and Mother drove up in the two-mule team.

Immediately the Indians drew back until they had regained their horses, which were being held meanwhile by the other members of the party.

Father was out of the wagon in a twinkling, with a pistol in each hand and coming rapidly toward me, shouting for those in the rear to hurry on, as if he had a large company at his back.

The Indians did not wait to learn how strong we were in numbers, and more than likely they saw the cloud of dust in the distance which told of the coming of the cattle and the loaded wagons; perhaps they believed it was raised by a troop of men, for without parley, and before one could have counted ten, they had wheeled about and were riding at their best pace in the opposite direction.

So great was my relief of mind that I felt inclined

to make light of the adventure, but was straightway sobered when Father said gravely:—

"There is much to be feared from those Comanches. The only reason I have not already cautioned you often and very strongly is because I feared to alarm your mother. Do not take any chances if, when you are alone, you come upon such as those who have just fled, but seek safety in flight if possible. If you cannot escape, make ready for a desperate defense, and even when you are on our claim, have your weapons always ready for use."

So intent had I been in planning what might be

done in raising sheep, that the possibility of having trouble with the Indians never came into my mind; but now that Father had spoken as he did, I knew that beyond a doubt there was good reason for caution, if not for alarm.

Straightway my thoughts went out into the future, as I asked myself how it would be possible, while herding sheep, to defend myself, for I well understood that only Gyp and I could be spared to play the part of shepherds. All the others would be attending to the regular work of the ranch, and could not be expected to give heed to me.

# THE ARRIVAL AT FORT TOWSON

I was still turning this unpleasant prospect over in my mind when we arrived at Fort Towson, and then I began to believe the country of Texas was not all I had fancied. It was only reasonable for a lad like me to expect that at this fort I would find something which resembled a fortification, and yet, so far as could be judged from the outside, it was no more than the ordinary buildings of a ranchman, except that walls of sun-dried bricks connected the several structures, forming a square. On the side facing the south were two heavy gates of logs, which now swung wide open, but it was plain to be seen that they could be closed quickly if need arose.

There were in charge of this ranchlike fort no more than six or seven men, and of these, two were Mexicans, while all wore the same clothing that may be seen in every Spanish settlement.

## PREPARING FOR A STORM

It was yet early in the afternoon when we came to this halting place. We had no reason to complain of our reception, for the man who appeared to be the leader of the company came out even before we were ready to enter the enclosure, and said, while John and Zeba were driving the cattle to what seemed good pasturage, that it would be better for us if we herded the stock inside the fort.

This caused me some surprise, for since early morning the air had been so calm that a feather would not have been blown from a tree top, and the weather was warm and sultry, giving promise of discomfort if one were shut within the four walls of the fort.

I fancy even Father was astonished because the man invited us inside when it was almost suffocatingly hot on the open prairie. Seeing that we hesitated, the leader of the small garrison pointed toward the west, where could be seen a few low-hanging, sluggish clouds drifting slowly here and there, while at the same time I thought I saw a yellow smudge low down on the northern horizon.

"It's a norther," the man said as if believing he had

explained matters sufficiently. When Father still hesitated, he added, "Your cattle will be stampeded when the wind comes, unless you have them corralled, and there is not time for you to get the wagons in position."

I did not understand even then, for I had never been told anything whatsoever regarding these strange storms which are called "northers" by Texans, but I noticed that Father ran at full speed to give orders for John and Zeba to turn the cattle into the fort, and as he went he shouted for me to herd the sheep within the enclosure.

The man who had bidden us welcome aided me in the task, and more than that, for when the sheep were snugly inside, he ran back to tell the drivers of the wagons to get their mules unhooked and in a safe place before the wind came.

## A DRY "NORTHER"

We were hardly more than thus housed before a distant roaring could be heard, not unlike thunder, and in a short time the wind was upon us in a perfect hurricane, cold as icy water.

At one instant the perspiration had been running down my face because of the exertion of hurrying the sheep and mules into the fort, and in the next I felt as if I had taken a plunge into a bank of snow.

My teeth chattered as I followed the Mexicans, who were running into one of the buildings, and I noticed, as I went at full speed, that the mules and the cattle had turned tail to the storm of wind, standing with lowered heads, as such beasts are wont to do during a tempest.

There was no rain, but a sort of mist hung in the air, which soon gave way to a blue haze, and I fancied it had a peculiar odor, like the smoke from burning straw. I paid no great attention to it at the time, however, so eager was I to come to the heat of the fire, which had been speedily built in that hut to which the Mexicans fled for refuge.

It was while I stood there striving to get some comfort from the cheery blaze, that the leader of the company came into the room. Joining me at the fireplace, and knowing of course by this time that I was having my first experience with a Texan "norther," he explained to me the peculiarity of these storms, which, as I found out later, are frequent in these regions.

# CHAPTER
# FIVE

---

## TWO KINDS OF "NORTHERS"

The Texans divide the storms into what they call a wet, and a dry, norther.

Wet northers are those which bring rain or sleet, and usually last twelve or fourteen hours without doing any particular damage, ending with a mild north or northwest wind. But the stock is likely to suffer from the storms, because of being wet with the sleet or rain, and then thoroughly chilled by that ice-cold wind.

The dry norther I have already told about. Our host explained to me that it might continue fiercely for from twenty-four to forty-eight hours, then gradually

die away in from twelve to eighteen hours, during all
of which time that penetrating cold would continue.

I soon came to understand that the man had told
no more than the truth, for Father said, when he finally came where I was, that we should probably have
to remain penned up in Fort Towson two or three
days, and advised me to make myself as comfortable
as possible, for we were welcome to the use of any of
the buildings.

The only way in which I could follow this advice
was to hug the fire as closely as possible, for whenever
I moved a short distance away, that chilling air would
envelop me as if with a mantle of ice, and I thought
to myself more than once, that if I were to be caught
out on the prairie herding a flock of sheep when one
of these northers came up, I might freeze to death.

I did, however, venture away from the heat long
enough to make certain that my mother was comfortable. There were two other women in the fort, one
a Mexican who appeared to be a sort of servant, and
the other the wife of that man who had extended to
us the hospitality of the place. With these two my
mother remained nearly forty hours, when the wind
subsided and the air grew balmy once more.

I remained the greater portion of that time in the

hut where I first sought refuge. The hours were not wasted, for I had a strong desire to learn something regarding this country in which we were to make our new home.

Before the storm cleared away, but when the wind had so far subsided that one might venture out without fear of freezing to death, a big wagon train came up toward the fort, evidently expecting to pass the night there. Then for the first time I saw those people who freight goods from the Missouri River down into Texas and Mexico form with their wagons what they call a corral. It was to me something well worth watching, even though I might have been more comfortable inside the building in front of a blazing fire.

# MAKING A CORRAL OF WAGONS

The train was made up of heavy wagons, each drawn by four yoke of cattle. When the first came up in front of the fort, the driver turned his team at an angle with the trail, bringing the oxen away from the fort and the rear end of the wagon toward it.

The second wagon was wheeled around within a short distance of the first, the intention of the teamsters being to halt the heavy carts in such positions that when all had arrived a circle would be formed, within which the cattle could be kept. On that side nearest the fort a passage between two of the wagons, five or six feet in width, was left open through which the oxen could be driven after they had been unyoked.

As soon as the cattle had been taken to where they might feed, heavy ropes were stretched across the opening, so that the four mules which had been driven by the owners of the train were actually fenced in, and there was no need either to hobble or to make them fast with a picket line, for they could not make their way out between the wagons.

It was all done in a way which showed that these people had been accustomed to making camp quickly so that they would have a place where they might corral the stock, and stand some chance of defending themselves against Indians.

It was this precaution on the part of the teamsters which gave me yet more reason than I had on meeting the Comanches to understand that in this country there were many chances that we might be called upon to battle for our lives.

One of the drivers told me that, on the march, when a norther springs up, they always make a corral in this fashion, forming it sufficiently large to herd all the cattle within the circle. If they are not sharply looked after, the animals will take to their heels as if frightened out of their wits. Therefore people who are accustomed to such sudden changes in the weather are ever on the lookout lest their cattle be left where they may not readily be bunched. Oxen will become wilder through fear of a norther than they can be made through the shrieking and yelling of Indians who are trying to stampede them.

# ON THE TRAIL ONCE MORE

On the second morning after our arrival at Fort Towson we set off once more, Father and Mother leading the way in the small mule cart, and I following behind the three wagons, while John and Zeba brought up the rear with the cattle, which, having had a welcome rest at the fort, were now traveling at a reasonably rapid pace, so fast, in fact, that Gyp and I had to urge the sheep along at their best speed lest we be overrun.

At the end of the first day's journey Father told me that we had crossed over the border line of the republic, and were then in Texas. This was pleasing news, because the long journey had become decidedly wearisome.

# MESQUITE

During the day we had been traveling over rolling land, which was covered with rich grass and looked not unlike what I have heard about the ocean, for we climbed over billow after billow and saw the same sea of undulating green stretched out before us, with here and there a small clump of oak or pecan trees, or thickets of mesquite.

Mesquite, of which there is so much in Texas, sometimes grows to the height of thirty or forty feet, but as a rule it is found as bushes no more than five or six feet high. It bears a pod something like a bean, which, before ripening is soft and exceedingly sweet, and so very pleasant to the taste that white people as well as Indians gather it as fruit. The wood of the mesquite, which may be found reasonably large in size, and which is of a brown or red color when polished, but exceedingly hard to work, is valuable for the underpinnings of houses, for fence posts, and even for furniture.

The next morning after we had crossed the Texas line we came upon the very thing in which I had the greatest interest, a sheep ranch, and I urged Father to halt there for an hour or more that I might see how the animals were cared for here in this country, as compared with our manner of feeding and housing them in Mississippi.

# CHAPTER
# SIX

———

## A TEXAS SHEEP RANCH

Save for the house in which the shepherds live, I saw very little in the way of buildings for sheltering the stock. There were immediately around the dwelling (which, by the way was made partly of sun-dried brick and partly of mesquite wood) twenty or thirty small sheep pens, with cribs inside formed of rails loosely laid together, the whole looking as if some indolent person had decided to start in the sheep-raising business with as little labor as possible.

The only person we could see on the ranch was a man who acted as cook. Fortunately for me, he appeared more than willing to answer the many questions I was eager to ask. In the first place, he told me, as others had, that the northern part of Texas was not adapted to sheep raising in comparison with the western, or the panhandle, section, but that the owners of the ranch were making a very profitable business out of it just at that time.

They had four herders for about five thousand sheep. Each herder had a dog, and with his dog he remained out on the range month after month, being allowed so many lambs or sheep every thirty days for his own food. The two were supplied by the cook with the other things they might need, such as flour, a bit of bacon, and salt. The wages paid at that time were only twenty dollars a month.

# THE PROFITS FROM SHEEP RAISING

The cook had some marvelous stories to tell of the money that might be made in Texas by sheep raising, and among them was this:—

A man for whom he worked received as a net profit from a flock of only fifteen hundred sheep seventeen hundred dollars, which is almost as well as he could have done in Mississippi.

Even though I had not been bent on sheep raising before we entered Texas, that story alone would have been sufficient to excite my desire to engage in it. It is true my twelve sheep would make a sorry showing by the side of fifteen hundred, but yet I was only twelve

years old, and, as I had said to myself again and again, fortune must go against me exceedingly hard if by the time I had come to manhood I could not show more than fifteen hundred, even though the beginning had been so small.

# FATHER'S LAND CLAIM

After seeing that sheep ranch and hearing the stories told of the money that might be made in the business,

I was more eager than ever to come to that claim which Father had staked out, so I might get my share of the flock in good condition while we were building our home, and there was no portion of the journey that seemed so long and so wearisome to me as the eight and forty hours after we left the ranch. Then we came to the location of our new home, and had it not been for that experience with the dry norther, I would have said that in such a spot a lad might live until he was gray-headed, with never a desire to leave.

# THE CHAPARRAL COCK

Father's claim was in a valley where was a large motte, or grove, of pecan trees. As we came up to the place a bird called a chaparral cock looked down on me with what I fancied was a note of welcome. It seemed to me a happy sign that the little fellow should have uttered his cry at the very moment my eyes rested upon him.

His head was cocked on one side, and his black, beady eyes twinkled in a most kindly fashion, so that I hailed him as a friend and vowed that neither he nor any of his family should come to harm through me unless it might be that we were sorely pressed for food. But it did not appear to me probable we should ever be put to such straits as that of killing a bird who thus made us welcome.

Father had already decided upon the location of the house, which was to be just south of the pecan trees, which would shelter us from those icy northers. The three wagons and the two-mule cart were therefore drawn up side by side at the very spot where he intended to build the dwelling, so that we might use them for lodgings until we had a better place.

# OUR FIRST NIGHT ON THE TRINITY

The livestock were turned out that night to wander as they would. We had no fear of their straying, for since leaving Fort Towson all the animals had been pushed forward at their best pace, and every one was sufficiently weary to remain near at hand.

Before darkness had come we learned that the little chaparral cock was not the only neighbor we were to have in our new home, for there came from the distance what sounded like screams of pain, and sharp, yelping barks. The hair stood up on Gyp's back, and he bared his teeth as if ready for a most desperate struggle, while I took good care to keep him close beside me as I tumbled into the two-mule cart for my rifle, not knowing what danger threatened us.

Then Father laughed heartily and told me that the dismal, blood-curdling noises which I heard came from a pack of coyotes, or wolves, howling, perhaps in expectation of getting supper. He predicted that we would soon become accustomed to such disagreeable noises, for there was little doubt but that these beasts would remain our neighbors until we could kill them off, or, at least, make them afraid of venturing near our clearing.

A large part of the goods was thrown out of the wagons that we might spread our beds in comfort, for it was expected that we should live under the canvas coverings until we had built our house; the first work necessary was the setting up of some kind of shanty to serve as a cook room.

That night, however, a fire was built in the open, and over it Mother prepared the evening meal while Father and I milked the cows. With smoking hot corn bread, fried bacon, bacon fat in which to dip the bread, and plenty of fresh milk, we had such a meal as tired emigrants could fully appreciate.

# STANDING GUARD

If I imagined that all of us were to lie down in the wagons and take our rest on this first night after arriving at the Trinity, I was very much mistaken. Father made me forget all about sleep and rest, when he said that unless we kept sharp watch against the coyotes we were likely to lose several sheep before morning, and that it was necessary that at least two of us stand guard throughout the night.

If only the oxen or the mules had been in danger, perhaps I would not have been so eager to shoulder my rifle and, in company with Zeba, tramp around and around the animals until midnight. As it was, however, I did my duty faithfully, and when the night was half spent, Father came out with John to relieve us. I was so weary that when I crawled into one of the wagons on to the soft feather bed, it seemed to me as if my legs would drop from my body, and my eyes were so heavy with slumber that it was only by the greatest exertion I could keep them open.

When next I was conscious of my surroundings, the rising sun was sending long yellow shafts of light beneath the canvas covering of the wagon; the little chaparral cock was calling out from the pecan motte near at hand, as if to assure me he still stood my friend; while far away could be heard the shrieks, yelps, and barks of the cowardly wolves which had been sneaking around our flock of sheep all night.

# CHAPTER
# SEVEN

---

## A TURKEY BUZZARD

I came out of the wagon with a bound, determined that from this on until I had my flock of five thousand sheep, there should be no dallying on my part.

As I started toward the stream for a morning bath, a big black shadow came between me and the sun. Looking up, I saw for the first time a turkey buzzard, his black coat and red crest showing vividly against the sky as he flapped lazily in front of me to alight in the near vicinity of the chaparral cock. I was so superstitious as to believe for the moment that the sudden appearance of this disagreeable-looking bird at the very moment when the little cock was bidding

me good morning, threatened disaster to our scheme of making a home and to my plan of raising sheep.

With the air fresh and bracing, the sunlight flooding everything with gold, and even with the dismal shrieks and yelps in the distance, it would have been a pretty poor kind of fellow who could have remained long disheartened, simply because a grumbling old turkey buzzard chanced to fly in front of him.

The stream by the side of which I hoped to live for many a long year was not deep at this season, but clear as crystal, and just cool enough to give me the sensation of being keenly alive when I plunged in head foremost. I floundered about until I heard

Mother calling for me to hurry while the corn bread was hot, lest I lose my share, for both she and Father were ravenously hungry.

While we ate we decided where the cook camp should be put up and how we would care for the cattle, the sheep, and the mules while we were building our house. In fact, very many plans were laid during those ten or fifteen minutes, some of which were carried out at once.

# PLANS FOR BUILDING A HOUSE

As for the cook shanty, we were not inclined to spend very much time over it. Simply a shelter from the dew and the sun, where Mother might be screened from the wind, so she could use the cookstove we had brought with us, was all we needed.

Father intended to build a house of lumber, even though at that time he knew that he would be forced to pay anywhere from twenty to thirty dollars a thousand feet for cheap boards, and then haul them no less than two hundred miles.

After he had told me about the lumber I asked in wonder and surprise if he counted on spending so much money, when we might build a house as the Mexicans do, of adobe brick, with no more timber in it than would serve to hold up a roof of mud. He laughingly replied that when we had made a saw pit, he would show me how we might get out our own building material, and said that I was to have a hand in the manufacture, for he thought I could do my share of the sawing when I was not looking after the cattle or the sheep.

Before leaving home he had made arrangements to keep with us the three slaves whom we had hired in Bolivar County, until we were fairly settled. Therefore we had seven pairs of hands in this house building, which should put the work along in reasonably rapid fashion, even though five of the laborers were not skilled.

We spent no more time at breakfast than was necessary for eating and for roughly sketching out the plans for the day's work. After this each set about his task. I drove the sheep a short distance away toward the farther end of the valley, where they could conveniently get at the water and yet find rich pasturage; John and Zeba picketed out the mules; and Father with the three hired men rounded up the cattle.

## THE COOK SHANTY

This done, we set about making a shanty by digging to the depth of two or three feet a space about three yards wide and four yards long, around the sides of which we set branches of pecan trees. We planted poles at the four corners so that we could use the wagon covers for walls and roof.

When this rudest kind of rude building was so far finished that it would screen us from the wind, we set up the cookstove, and Mother began what in Bolivar County she would have called her regular Saturday's baking. After this we put on a roof of canvas, pinning the whole down as best we might with mesquite bushes, until we had a shed which would serve, but which was most crude looking.

Although there was nothing on which we could pride ourselves in this first building, it had occupied us nearly the entire day, and I had no more than an

hour in which to rest my weary limbs before it was necessary to stand guard over the sheep, lest the wolves carry off the beginnings of my flock.

It was during this night, when it cost not only great effort, but real pain, to keep continually on the move lest I fall asleep, that I decided that at the very first opportunity I would build a corral. While our flock was so small, it would not be a very great task to build a pen sufficiently large to hold the animals together, and at the same time shut out the wolves. There were enough mesquite bushes, or trees, to provide me with the necessary material, and I decided upon the place where I would build a pen, figuring in my mind how the work could be best done.

Therefore, when Father relieved me at midnight, I had in my mind's eye the first sheep pen put up on the West Fork of the Trinity, and already in imagination was on the high road to prosperity.

# A STORM OF RAIN

When another morning came, my dreams of what the future might bring me had become decidedly cloudy, for the rain was falling, not furiously, as in the case of a norther or a short-lived tempest, but with a steady downfall which told of a long spell of disagreeable weather, and I was not the only member of our party to come out from the beds in the wagons looking disheartened, and uncomfortably damp.

At our old home in Bolivar County the first sound

in the morning which usually broke upon my ear was that of Mother's singing as she prepared breakfast. On this day she was in our cook house, but working in silence. So, forgetting my own discomfort in the fear that something might have gone wrong with her, I asked why I had not heard her morning song. In reply she pointed first to the heavens, and then

to our stock of household belongings, which were strewn here and there where they had been taken from the wagons. To give her cheer, I tried to laugh, saying there was little among our goods which would come to harm because of the rain, and such as might be injured I would quickly get under cover. She replied in an injured tone that Father had told her there were few rainstorms in Texas during the year, save when a norther raged.

# A DAY OF DISCOMFORT

I ventured to jest with her, by saying most likely it had been arranged for our especial benefit, as we were newcomers in the country and needed to be introduced to all varieties of climate. The light words failed to bring a smile to her lips. So, without loss of time, I set about carrying such of our belongings as might be injured by the rain to the shelter of the wagons, and had hardly more than begun the task when Father returned, his face quite as gloomy as Mother's.

He tried to apologize for this sort of weather, and began by saying that from all he had learned during his first visit there was little danger that we should be visited by a very long storm.

Everyone was out of humor, and although the morning was not cold, all were shivering, and looked as if they had been taking a bath in the stream. I asked Zeba what had happened. In sulky tones he told me that while he had been rounding up the cattle and bunching them at the upper end of the

valley, so that they would not stray too far on the prairie, he had been treated to a veritable shower bath from the moisture on the mesquite bushes and the pecan trees.

# CHAPTER
# EIGHT

---

## THINKING OF THE OLD HOME

The chaparral cock was silent. Even the turkey buzzard had forsaken the pecan motte. The mules, which I could see in the distance, were hanging their long ears dejectedly, and the cattle in a most forlorn manner stood humped up with their heads away from the wind. Only the sheep grazed with seeming contentment.

When I went into the cook camp, in order to get my breakfast, I was thinking of the old plantation in Bolivar County, where, when it rained, we had good shelter instead of being homeless in the wilderness, as one might say.

And surely we were in a wilderness, there on the

banks of the Trinity, exposed to all the downpour, save when we crawled into one of the wagons to shelter ourselves while Mother continued her work. There is no need that I should say the breakfast was inviting, for my mother could cook the meanest of food in such a manner that it would appeal to one's appetite, yet we ate as if it were a duty rather than a pleasure to break our fast after so much watching.

When the meal was ended, Father set the men to gathering up the remainder of our goods that might be injured by dampness, and I, rather than remain idle when there was so much work to be done, took part in the task, until we had nearly everything sheltered.

The only places of refuge against the storm were the miserable shanty we had put up so hastily and the small two-mule wagon in which Father and Mother had ridden.

We were a mournful-looking company of emigrants, when, the last of the goods having been stowed away, we sat under one of the wagon bodies, while Mother continued to work in the shanty regardless of the rain which came in through a hundred crevices.

## WAITING FOR THE SUN

The slaves gathered about Father and me, in order to take advantage of the shelter afforded by the wagon. We remained silent a full ten minutes before Father strove to cheer our spirits by suggesting that a storm at this season of the year could not last very many hours, and that by the following morning we should be rejoicing in the heat and the brightness of the sun.

He was at fault in this prediction, however. During the remainder of the day we came out from the shelter now and then to make certain that the cattle, the mules, and the sheep yet remained within the valley, and then crept back once more to keep mournful silence, seldom breaking it, save when the meals were ready.

The rain continued to fall steadily, and yet it was necessary we stand guard against the coyotes, who began to howl, and scream, and bark as soon as night came. No longer dreaming of making my fortune at sheep raising, I went off with Zeba just before darkness covered the earth, to begin the weary march around and around our herd of cattle and flock of sheep. I was soon drenched to the skin, and wished that Father had never been attacked by the Texas fever.

I wondered during that long, wet, disagreeable time of watching where the other newly arrived settlers had begun to make homes in Texas. I knew that hundreds of families near us in Bolivar County, and from Kentucky and Missouri, had come into this Republic of Texas, and it seemed, as I thought it over, most singular that we had failed to meet with any of them.

The storm, the darkness, and the irritating calls of the coyotes had so worked upon my mind that I came to believe that all the stories we had heard of people who were to make homes in this new country had been false. It seemed to me that we were the only persons in the United States who had been so foolish as to venture across the Red River with wild dreams of fertile ranches and rapidly increasing herds of cattle or flocks of sheep.

# TOO MUCH WATER

Three days passed before we again rejoiced in the light of the sun. During that time so much discomfort and actual danger had been met that I was sick at heart at the very sound of the name of Texas.

Before the end of the second day we had succeeded in making the cook shanty nearly waterproof, by stripping all the wagons of their covers, and pinning the canvas down over the pecan branches. This left our goods exposed to the rain, and many of our belongings were necessarily ruined, although we took little heed of that fact, if only it was possible to give Mother some degree of comfort.

On the morning of the third day the valley was dotted here and there with pools of water, showing that the soil had drunk its fill and refused to take in more. In order to move about in the valley, it was necessary at times to wade ankle-deep. The result was that Father and I, as well as the other men, were forced to wear garments saturated with water, since it would have been useless to put on dry clothes, for after an hour of tramping to and fro they would have been in the same wet condition. Yet we had no thought of real danger. There was in our minds simply the painful idea that we must endure what could not be avoided; we never dreamed that worse was to come.

## THE STREAM RISING

Just before time for dinner on the third day I noticed that the sheep were making their way rapidly up out of the valley, and, fearing lest they might stray so far that it would be impossible to herd them before nightfall, I followed, leaving Father and the other men crouching under one of the wagon bodies.

To my surprise, when I had walked a few yards from where we were encamped, I found the water in many of the pools nearly ankle-deep, and saw that the western side of the valley, that part farthest from the stream, was literally flooded.

Strange as it may seem, neither Father nor I had given any particular heed to the rising of the stream. There was in our minds, dimly perhaps, an idea that the amount of water had increased during this long storm, and we were not disquieted on seeing it come up to the height of the banks; but now, being warned by the depth of water in the valley, I quite forgot the sheep for an instant, and ran back to where I could have a full view of the river.

The flood was already overlapping the banks at the northern end of the valley, a fact which accounted for the quantity of water I had found while going toward the sheep, and I fancied it was possible to hear, far away in the distance, a roaring noise such as a waterfall might produce.

# CHAPTER
# NINE

---

## TRYING TO SAVE THE STOCK

Heedless of the fact that my twelve sheep were stam-peded, I ran swiftly along the edge of the stream toward the wagons, shouting wildly that a flood was upon us. I was yet twenty or thirty yards distant when Father came out to learn why I was raising such an alarm.

It needed but one glance for him to understand that we were in the gravest danger. Even while I ran, it was possible for me to see the river rising, rising, until what, at the moment I set off to herd the sheep, had been comparatively dry land, was being flooded so rapidly that before I had gained the wagons, they were standing a full inch deep in the water.

Father ran hurriedly, with a look of alarm on his face, toward the cook shanty and shouted for Mother to make all haste, to leave everything behind her, and to clamber into one of the wagons. Then, turning to the other men, he literally drove them out from their shelter, ordering them to round up the mules without delay so we might hitch them to the wagons. It was not necessary that I should be told to obey this command on the instant, even though it was not directed to me. I wheeled about, intending to turn the mules in the direction of the wagons, leaving the other men to bring up the harness, but while doing so, I saw that we were too late by at least three or four minutes, for the mules, having already taken alarm by the rising of the water, were making their way at a quick pace up the incline which led to the higher land, following directly behind the sheep.

# THE ANIMALS STAMPEDED

Probably, if I had moved more cautiously, I might have circled around them, and thus checked their flight until the others could come up; but I was so thoroughly alarmed by the rapid rise of the water and the ominous roaring in the distance, that I set off at full speed directly toward the animals, and in a twinkling they broke into a gallop, stampeding the sheep by plunging among them.

As if this was not sufficient disaster, the cattle, which had been feeding fully a mile farther down the valley, now wheeled suddenly about in alarm, and set off over the ridge, bellowing with fear, their tails swinging high in the air.

So unreasoning was I in the sudden fright which had come upon me, that I failed to realize it would be useless to pursue any of our livestock, until Father shouted for me to turn back without loss of time. His voice, even though he was no more than two hundred yards away, came dimly to my ears because of the increasing roar in the distance, which sounded more and more threatening each instant.

When I gathered my wits about me sufficiently to obey the command, I saw that he, with the other men, was striving desperately to haul one of the heavy wagons from the bank of the stream; but so sodden with water was the earth that the wheels sank into the soft surface to the depth of two or three inches, and, struggle as they might, it could not be moved a single pace.

## SAVING OUR OWN LIVES

"Gather up the spare clothing, and take your mother with you!" Father shouted as I came up to where the black men were standing by the side of the wagon they had so vainly attempted to haul. I cried out dully, overcome with fear, asking where I should go with Mother; but even while speaking, I had sufficient common sense remaining to pull out from among our belongings as many water-soaked garments as I could get my hands on.

"Go to the high land!" Father shouted, and literally dragged Mother out from her seat in the wagon, where she had been crouching since the water flooded the cook camp. She had her wits about her sufficiently to understand what Father would have us do. Calling on me to follow, she took from my arms a portion of the burden and set off straight across that increasing flood of water in the direction taken by the animals. She realized that they, prompted by instinct, would lead the way to the highest point of land.

Thus we two, Mother and I, abandoned Father and all our belongings, and it surely seemed as if we were leaving him to a terrible fate. I would have come to a full stop in order to urge him to follow us, but Mother called out that I should not slacken pace. She said that he knew better than we what should be done, and that he would follow without loss of time.

It seemed to me that we had no sooner gained the top of the bank, and from there the highest point of one of the prairie hills, when, looking around, I saw Father and the other men coming at full speed, as if fleeing from death itself. And this really was the case, as I saw a few seconds later. I would have run toward the edge of the valley in the hope of helping them, but Mother held me back.

# A RAGING TORRENT

The roar of the coming flood was deafening. Father and the others were yet clambering up the side of the valley when I saw, coming down the channel of the river, a raging torrent which bore on its surface trunks of trees such as would have dealt death to any one who might have been in their line of advance. On the waters were fragments of wood, bunches of mesquite bushes, and I fancied now and then the body of an ox; but it was all a scene of confusion, of noise, and of menace.

During perhaps ten seconds I felt certain Father would be swept away by the raging stream which was filling the valley. The torrent swelled until the crest of the muddy waves swept against Zeba's legs, for he was the last of that little company struggling to save his life. Not one moment too soon did Father and the other men gain the high land. They were hardly in safety when all our valley was filled with water, and

I knew that beneath the flood was everything we owned in the world save the livestock.

Father came swiftly on until he stood by Mother's side, clasping both her hands. But he spoke not a word, and I realized that we had come from Bolivar County with all our belongings only to have them swept away, and that we were destitute.

As I saw a huge pecan tree, tossing and rolling on the brown waves, I asked myself if such a monster could be thrown about like a straw, what must become of our wagons in the valley?

# A TIME OF DISASTER

It was much like mockery to see the clouds breaking away immediately after all the mischief had been done. Before we had been upon the high land ten minutes the clouds gave way here and there, until we could see a glint of the sun. The rain ceased falling, and he would have been a poor weather prophet indeed who could not have foretold that the long storm had come to an end; but, as I said bitterly to myself, it had brought with it the end of all our dreams.

The cattle, mules, and sheep had stampeded. Far away in the distance I could see that little flock of mine, and yet farther beyond them, barely to be distinguished by the naked eye, were the cattle.

The mules had disappeared entirely, and I, who was ignorant of a ranchman's work, believed for the moment that we had seen the last of every head of stock and that we could never round them up again.

I looked to see Father overwhelmed with sorrow, and, therefore, great was my surprise when I heard him say cheerily:—

"It is well that we had this experience early in our Texan life, else the disaster might have been greater. Now we know it would be in the highest degree unwise to build our home in the valley, for if the stream rises in flood once, it will again, and we might lose our lives. It will not require any great length of time for us to make good the damage that has been done."

It almost vexed me that he should speak so lightly of what seemed to me a disaster which could not be repaired. When I asked how matters might possibly be worse, he replied laughingly that we were still alive, our stock would not stray so far but that we could soon herd them up, and there were many things in the wagons which would not be seriously harmed by the wetting.

To this day I am inclined to believe he put the best face possible upon the matter, so that Mother might not grieve, and certainly his cheery words helped us all. What was more to the purpose, the fact that he set each one some task to perform prevented us from dwelling upon the possibilities of the future.

# CHAPTER
# TEN

---

## THE FLOOD SUBSIDING

The storm had cleared away like magic; within half an hour from the time our valley was flooded and the rain had ceased falling, the sun was shining brightly. The waters were no longer rising, and I did not need Father to tell me they must, as a matter of course, subside quite as quickly as they had come.

Already I fancied that the tide was falling and that the torrent swept past with less force. I would have stood idly watching it, but that Father insisted I should go with him and the other men to a motte of pecans a short distance away, there to set about putting up a shelter for Mother's comfort.

It was well we were forced to work to the utmost of our power, and so we did. When night came, Mother at least had a shelter over her head. The slaves and I were content to lie down anywhere beneath the mesquite bushes, and there we slept soundly as if no disaster had overtaken us. There was no need of standing guard against the wolves, for we no longer had anything save ourselves to watch over.

When I expressed my fear that the wolves might kill the greater number of our sheep, Father insisted that there was more than a possibility that all the flock would be found; and he promised that if any were killed during the night, he would make my loss good from his own share of the flock.

# A JACK RABBIT

When I awoke the first rays of the sun were falling through the mesquite bushes fairly upon my face. A jack rabbit, his long ears flapping comically as he humped across the prairie, stopped when he was nearly opposite the motte of pecans to wonder who these people were, who had come to disturb him. This was the first object to meet my gaze, and however great might have been the sorrow in my heart, I could not have kept from laughing long and loud at the ridiculous creature.

I soon saw, however, that his clownish appearance was not to be counted strongly against him, for, startled by my rising quickly, he darted away with the fleetness of a deer. I question whether, if my rifle had been at that moment in my hands ready for use, I could have done more than take aim before he was out of sight among the bushes.

Then came a cheery good morning, as I interpreted it, from a chaparral cock, and I fancied it was the same fellow who had welcomed us to the valley. Following this friendly morning greeting came the screaming of a bird which I afterward knew was called a killdeer. I was wondrously cheered by the sight and sounds of life around.

## REPAIRING DAMAGES

Then came the work of the day, the first for me being to build a fire, even though there was nothing to be cooked. It had been my duty at home in Bolivar County to perform this service, and unwittingly I did it then, not remembering the fact that all our provisions were at the bottom of that brown flood. Mother asked, as she came out from her poor shelter, why I thought it necessary to start a blaze. I looked dumbly back at the valley which we had left in such haste, and to my surprise saw the tops of the wagons just appearing above the surface of the water, so rapidly had the torrent subsided. Father said laughingly, as if it was a matter which amused him exceedingly:—

"We will wait for breakfast until we can get a side of bacon from one of the wagons, unless you, Philip, are inclined to dive beneath the water for one."

It was evident we were to have little to eat during that day if we depended upon rescuing anything eatable from the flood. So I suddenly determined

that I would not be outdone by Father in cheerful-
ness and proposed that John go with me in search
of the cattle.

"I am thinking all of us must take a hand in that
work," Father said. Then turning to Mother, he asked
if she would be willing to remain there among the pecan trees alone while we roamed the prairie in search
of the cattle.

It was a useless question, for my mother was a
woman who always stood ready to do that which
came to her hand, regardless of her own pleasure or
inclination.

# ROUNDING UP THE LIVESTOCK

We set off at once, hungry as we were, on what I thought would be a useless journey. I was prepared to tramp all day, if necessary, without getting sight of a single animal belonging to us, and yet, greatly to my surprise, an hour before noon we came upon the entire flock of sheep with never a one missing. They were feeding as peacefully as if they had been herded by a better shepherd than I ever claimed to be.

Gyp, who had kept close to my heels from the time the waters first came down upon us, now seemed to recover his spirits. For the first time since we had been forced to flee for our lives he gave vent to a series of joyful barks, running around and around the flock as if he had been ordered to do so.

Father proposed that Gyp and I return with the flock to where Mother was waiting, while he and the other men continued in search of the cattle and mules. Against this I was not inclined to make any protest, for it had worried me not a little because she was alone, although I failed to understand how any harm could come to her.

When the afternoon was about half spent, the men that Father had hired as mule drivers came in with all our herd of oxen and cows. They reported that Father, with John and Zeba, had kept on having seen the mules far away in the distance, and it was reasonable to suppose they would return to us before night had set in. This they did not do, however, and Mother and I were troubled because of their absence, yet we could do nothing but sit there, idly watching the sheep and gazing down now and then into the valley to mark the ebb of the waters.

# THE FIRST MEAL AFTER THE FLOOD

Half an hour before sunset, when the wagons stood out plainly in view, with the flood hardly more than up to their axles, I called upon the slaves to follow me, and we set out to look among our belongings for something to eat.

After searching about we came upon a side of bacon, which looked but little the worse for its long bath, save that it was coated in a most unpleasant fashion with mud. Thinking it impossible for us to find any other thing in condition for eating until after it had been well dried, we turned to the grove of pecans with our small prize.

I built a fire near where Mother's shelter of branches and leaves had been set up. Then from the mesquite bushes I cut twigs which would serve as forks to hold the meat in front of the blaze. After this I carved the bacon with the knife from my belt, and Mother broiled slice after slice, the savory odor causing me to realize how exceedingly hungry I was.

We ate heartily, almost greedily. When our hunger had been partly satisfied, we sat down to await the coming of Father, speculating upon his prolonged absence, until we had imagined that all sorts of evil had befallen him.

# CHAPTER
# ELEVEN

---

## WAITING FOR FATHER

He who crosses a bridge before he comes to it, or, in other words, the man or the lad who looks into the future for trouble, proves himself to be foolish, for all the worry of mind one may suffer will not change events by so much as a hair's breadth.

If Mother and I had remained there talking of this thing or of that which had happened in Bolivar County, and not looking out across the prairie with the idea that harm had befallen Father, then the evening might have been a pleasant one; but instead, we were almost distracted with fear, until about midnight, when the trampling of hoofs in the distance told us that the mules had been rounded up.

It seemed strange to me, when Father and the other men came into camp, bringing the mules with them, that in the stampede we had not lost a single animal. Every ox, cow, mule, and sheep that had been with us in the valley before the flood was now returned and herded in front of the pecan motte as peacefully as though nothing had occurred. But not far away we could hear the snarling, shrieking, and barking of the coyotes which served almost to

make it seem as if that flood had been no more than a disagreeable dream.

That night the hired men and I stood watch. Father, John, and Zeba had traveled so far afoot, and were so weary that I could not have the heart to rouse them when it came time for our relief from duty, and so we paced around the herds and flock until daylight.

When the first rays of the sun glinted all the foliage around us with gold, it was possible for me to look down into the valley from which we had fled, and get some slight idea of the misfortune that had overtaken us.

Because of the weight of the wagons, and owing to the fact that they were heavily laden with farming tools and such things as would not float, they had hardly been disturbed. Also, owing, I suppose, in a great degree, to their being sunk so far in the mud after the first onrush of the torrent, they had not been knocked about to any extent.

# RECOVERING OUR GOODS

As a matter of course everything, including the grass, was covered with mud; but the water, except here and there where it stood in small pools on the surface, had retreated to its proper place between the banks,

and there was nothing to prevent us from caring for
our goods.

Mother cooked all that was left of the bacon, after
which, with hunger still gnawing at our stomachs, we
went down to set our belongings to rights, and a wearisome day it was.

The harness of the mules had been swept down-
stream so far that we did not come upon any portion of it until the day was nearly done. Therefore,
we could not make any effort toward dragging the
wagons to the hard ground, but were forced to carry
in our hands every article which it was necessary to
spread out upon the clean grass to dry.

About nightfall, after having found enough harness for one team of mules, we succeeded in getting a single cart up to where Mother's camp had been made. Then it began to look as if we had really taken possession of this portion of Texas, for all around were spread clothing, bedding, household furniture, farming tools, and this thing and that which went to make up the cargo we had brought from Bolivar County.

The wagon covers which had been spread over our cook camp had floated down the stream beyond the possibility of our finding them before another day. Therefore, that night, my mother slept once more in her shelter of branches and leaves; Father and I made a bed for ourselves in the water-soaked wagon; and the other men, or such of them as were not on duty guarding the cattle, lay down on the ground beneath it.

# SETTING TO WORK IN GOOD EARNEST

From this on we had plenty with which to occupy our hands as well as our minds. There was ever the necessity of keeping the cattle rounded up, the sheep herded, and the mules from straying, and all this was the more difficult because they were now on the prairie instead of in the valley.

Father was determined that his first work in this new country should be the building of a house, and very shortly after the flood subsided, I understood what he meant, when he spoke of my taking a hand in getting out the lumber.

First, as a matter of course, we hauled the other wagons out of the valley, making a small corral with them near the pecan motte where we had decided to build a home. Then we hunted during a full day along the banks of the river for such of our belongings as had been carried away by the flood, and found everything of value before the search was ended.

Two of the men were told off to guard the flock and the herd. After the ground plan of our house was staked out, Father blazed such of the trees as he decided must be felled in order to provide us with lumber.

The men were set at work cutting these down, while Father made his preparations for that sawmill which amused me before it was finished, and caused my back and arms to ache sorely before it had fully served its purpose.

Roshel Robinson Elmer

## LABORING AT THE SAWMILL

Sheep herding is none too pleasant a task; but as compared with this hand sawmill of ours it seemed like positive pleasure. I said to myself that I would never again complain of the hardships of herding a

flock on no matter how large a range, because the memory of this method of working out lumber would always remain fresh in my mind.

I was not in the pit very many hours during the day. One of the hired men was called to take my place at intervals.

## WILD CATTLE

Before we had worked out by this slow process all the lumber that would be necessary for making our home, we were surprised to find that our herd of cattle had been increased by three handsome beasts, two cows and a bull, black as coals, with glistening, long, white horns.

They suddenly appeared among our herd, causing me, who first discovered them, the greatest possible surprise. It seemed almost like some work of magic that we should have gained these fellows without raising a hand. Thinking that they might be branded, as is the custom in Texas, I tried to come near enough to find out, but I soon understood that I might as well have tried to make close acquaintance with the shiest antelope that ever crossed the prairie.

These cattle were so wild that at the first sight of a man they would toss up their horns, bellow, and set off across the country with their tails raised high as a signal of danger, putting the very spirit of mischief into our cattle.

After making two or three vain attempts to come up with them, I realized that unless I would take the chances of stampeding our whole herd, I must leave them alone.

When I told Father of the wonderful discovery that we had grown the richer by three cattle, he treated the matter very calmly and explained the seeming mystery by saying that we were not the only persons who had found additions to their livestock, for during his first visit to Texas he had heard much concerning such cattle.

During the years from 1834 to 1836, when the Mexican army was retreating, the Indians ravaged the country between the Nueces and the Rio Grande to such extent that the Mexicans, owners and herds-men, abandoned their stock ranches, leaving behind them large herds of cattle which could not be carried away save at great risk, and these beasts had since then multiplied rapidly.

# CHAPTER
# TWELVE

---

## A DISAGREEABLE INTRUDER

The officers of the Texan army had been accustomed to send mounted men into the abandoned country, driving out the cattle for the use of the army and thus supplying the troops with meat at no other expense than that of searching for it, until there were no longer large herds to be seen. Now and then, however, as in our case, a ranchman would suddenly find three or four, or possibly a dozen, among his own herd.

Father was not much pleased at this addition to his stock, for those black fellows were so wild, having ranged the country as they willed during eight or ten years, that they played the mischief with the tame cattle, as I had already seen. At the slightest cause of alarm, they would set off in mad flight, and thus stampede the quietest herd that was ever rounded up.

"Tomorrow we will shoot that bull," Father said, "if it can be done without making too much trouble among our own cattle. Then perhaps the cows will quiet down a bit, and find it more agreeable to behave themselves than to run races across the prairie without cause."

Half an hour before daylight next morning Father and I, with plenty of ammunition, set off alone to do our best at cutting the wild bull out from the herd, and ending his career with a rifle ball.

We left our camp, without waiting for breakfast, believing in our ignorance that the hunt would not be long; but very shortly after it began we understood that we had more of a task on our hands than had been anticipated.

To get within rifle shot of the herd seemed for a long time an impossibility. No sooner would we come in sight of the animals than up would go their tails and away across the prairie all the cattle would dash as if suddenly grown wild.

# ODD HUNTING

Then it was necessary to creep up on them, stalking the huge creatures as carefully as we might have hunted deer; but so wild were they that the least incautious movement when we were creeping through the grass, wriggling along like snakes, would provoke a snort of terror, and away the whole herd would go again.

More than once I urged Father to turn back, saying we might drive our own cattle entirely across the Republic of Texas, and finally lose them, if we continued our efforts. I pointed out to him that already we were at least five or six miles from home and had not had our breakfast; but he replied grimly that if we would save our own stock, it was necessary to put an end to the career of that black bull, who seemed possessed by the spirit of mischief, or the tame cattle might grow so wild it would be impossible to herd them.

We made our way slowly at times, and again we ran swiftly if there was no danger of being seen by the beasts, for not less than fifteen miles, when we came to a pecan grove in which we hid ourselves, with the idea of resting from the exertion of the chase.

While we sat there concealed by the foliage, the very animal we were so eager to kill led the herd directly toward us. He kept on feeding leisurely twenty or thirty paces in advance of the others, and sniffing the air with each mouthful.

Fortunately for us the wind was blowing directly from him toward the pecan motte, and therefore he failed to scent any danger.

On he came, slowly at first, as handsome a beast as I ever saw. When he had ventured thus unsuspiciously within perhaps half a rifle shot, Father whispered to me that I should take careful aim, either at the bull's neck or just behind the fore shoulder, and when he gave the signal, I was to fire.

It seemed to me that the two shots rang out at the same instant, for they sounded like one, and the black bull pitched forward on his knees as if struck by lightning. A second later he had rolled over dead, and the work was finished, save the walk of fifteen miles before it would be possible to satisfy our hunger.

# A SUPPLY OF FRESH MEAT

We covered the carcass with the branches of the pecan trees as well as possible, in order to keep the wolves and the turkey buzzards away, for even though we had been here but a short time, I had learned that anything eatable left exposed on the prairie, particularly fresh meat, would soon be devoured by the noisy

coyotes or those unwholesome-looking birds. Then
we set out on our return to the home camp, leaving
the cattle to recover from the fright caused by the
report of our rifles as best they might.

When we arrived, at about three o'clock in the afternoon, Father set one of the men to harnessing two
mules to the small wagon, and announced that I was
to go back with a couple of the men to bring in our
game, for we could not well afford to lose so much
fresh meat.

The day had been a long one before I found opportunity to crawl into my bed, for it was near midnight when we got back with the carcass of the bull.

When I opened my eyes next morning, I remembered the saw pit, believing I must spend another day at the slow task of making boards and joists from green wood, but Father was at work cutting the carcass of the bull into thin strips, while John and Zeba were building a little scaffold on the prairie a short distance from Mother's shelter.

# "JERKING" BEEF

This was the first process towards "jerking" beef, or, in other words, drying it in the sun, a method of preserving meat which I fancy has come down to us from the Indians. Before the morning was spent I discovered that there are more disagreeable tasks than that of pushing a crosscut saw up and then pulling it down.

Before all the meat had been cut into thin ribbons and hung on the scaffolding, we were covered with blood, and on the topmost branches of the pecans sat a dozen or more of those miserable turkey buzzards, awaiting an opportunity to come down and eat what was left of the carcass. It was necessary to keep as close a watch over those birds as we did over the wolves, else all our labor would have been speedily devoured. When there was an opportunity for a much-needed bath, Father allowed no more than two of us to go into the stream at a time, obliging the others to remain where they might stand guard over the meat.

When night came, the ribbons of flesh were not wholly cured and we found it necessary to gather them up and store them in one of the wagons lest the dew spoil the flesh; in the morning we hung all the thin strips out again, standing over them jealously.

It seemed to me just then as if all our days and nights in Texas were to be spent standing guard over something. During the night we were forced to watch lest the wolves devour our sheep, and during the day we had to keep a careful eye over the turkey buzzards who seemed on the verge of starvation all the time. In addition to this labor, it was necessary to perform the regular work on the ranch, and thus it may be seen that we did not have much time for idling.

# CHAPTER
# THIRTEEN

## SEARCHING FOR THE CATTLE AGAIN

The next day Father sent out two of the men to search for our cattle, believing it would be useless for us to make any attempt at herding them until after they had had ample time to quiet down from the alarm caused by the chase and the killing of the bull.

The black men were absent from the camp twenty hours before coming back with all the herd. According to their story they traveled a long, long distance before coming upon the herd, and then they found it extremely difficult to drive the beasts in toward the Trinity River, because the two wild cows made every effort to stampede the herd whenever the men came in sight.

Perhaps I do not need to set down in detail all that we did during this first season on the Trinity, but I will tell what we accomplished.

# OUR NEW HOME

First, and next to the raising of sheep, the most important matter to me was the building of the house. This we did, working at odd times when not engaged

in planting, and seeing to it that never an hour was wasted, by any of us. When the work was finished, truly we had a building of which to be proud, for this new home seemed quite as fine as the one we had left in Bolivar County.

It was built throughout of sawed lumber; the roof

was made of a double thickness of boards, and the crevices on the sides of the house covered with the first strips taken from the trunks of the trees, with the bark still remaining; but this did not, in my eyes, detract from the general appearance of the whole.

Perhaps it was because I had labored so hard and so long on this home of ours, that it appeared so beautiful in my sight. At all events, it was most convenient, as even Mother admitted. We had one room on the front, overlooking the river, and back of that a storeroom and a kitchen, which, if not exactly fit for a king, served our purposes very well.

In the loft, which of course was directly under the roof, we had our beds, Mother, Father, and I. Just behind the building, or, I should say, on the other side of the pecan motte, was a small hut built of round logs for the two slaves. We had sent back on foot those men whom Father hired to drive the teams; therefore when our house was finished and the season at an end, only John and Zeba remained to aid in the labor of the ranch.

# PLANTING, AND BUILDING CORRALS

We had planted no less than three acres of corn and potatoes, all of which promised a bountiful harvest, and gave token of yielding two or three times as much as we could have hoped for on the richest of the Mississippi bottoms.

In addition to the dwellings, we had built a large pen for the sheep, made of mesquite bushes stuck so firmly into the ground that the coyotes would not dare attempt to force a passage through.

We also had smaller pens for the sheep with lambs, perhaps a dozen or more of them; for, as you know, the mother sheep very often will not take kindly to her young, and it is necessary either to tie her up, or put her in some small enclosure with the little fellow, during two or three days, until she becomes acquainted with him and is willing to admit that he belongs to her.

During the season the last work done by the slaves was the splitting of rails. With these and with the wagons, we made a corral for the mules, where they could be enclosed at night, or whenever there was promise of a norther which might stampede them. For those fierce storms came, as it seemed to me, very often.

# BAR-O RANCH

As for the oxen and cows, they were still allowed to roam over the prairie. We could not well provide them with a corral, because cattle often feed at night, and must have plenty of room in which to roam; but we took good care that they were branded, Father using as his mark a big letter O with a line drawn across the middle.

Because of this brand I decided we would call our new home the Bar-O Ranch, and to-day I venture to say it is as well known in the state of Texas as any other, even though we may not number our cattle by the thousands, as do the more wealthy cattle raisers.

During all that season we had but two visitors, and how they chanced to stray down our way so far off the trail I was curious to learn. They were Mexicans, each driving a cart of home manufacture.

# THE VISITORS

These Mexicans, who were driving two oxen to each cart, claimed to be going to Fort Towson after certain goods which were to be left there for them; but I doubted the statements made, as did Father, for they had their unwieldy vehicles partly filled with packages five or six feet long, wrapped in what looked like tow cloth, and we afterward learned that these were probably muskets being sent to the northern border to be sold to the Indians.

These strangers were decked out in most fanciful costumes, with scarf-like blankets of gaudy colors thrown over their shoulders, simply by way of ornament. They could speak only a few words of English, making their wants known mostly by gestures.

They asked if they might make camp near our house. Such a request was not to be refused, for they might have done as they pleased. Father would not have had the heart to drive them away, for the prairie, even though staked out as a homestead, is free to all travelers.

## ZEBA'S CURIOSITY

That evening Zeba's curiosity, like my own, was aroused by the sight of those bundles in the carts, which seemed heavy, as could be told when the Mexicans unyoked the oxen. He therefore loitered around trying to find an opportunity of learning what was inside the wrappings of tow; but before he succeeded in getting his hands on one of the packages, the Mexican drove him away with threats that I fancy would have been blood-curdling had we understood the Spanish language.

Their behavior toward Zeba, who thus far had done no more than stand idly by the side of one of the carts looking in, caused Father to suspect that their approaching Fort Towson by way of the West

Fork of the Trinity was not an accident, but rather done by design, that they might avoid the beaten lines of travel.

Therefore during the night that they remained in camp near us, both he and I stood guard, for while we had not heard very much concerning the troubles with Mexicans and Indians which the settlers on the western border were having, we knew the people of Mexico had no good will toward us who came from the States.

## POSSIBLE TREACHERY

On thinking it over, there appears to be good reason why the natives should be the enemies of those who have settled in Texas, for this republic was forcibly taken from the Mexican government at the cost of much bloodshed, and it would be strange indeed if they looked upon us in a friendly manner after that.

Even if they had not had so much territory taken from them, the Mexicans surely had good reason for unfriendliness when they remembered the battle of San Jacinto, to say nothing of the other engagements which gave independence to the Republic of Texas.

Father has always held that when the Comanche Indians overran Texas in 1840, they were urged on by the Mexicans, who hoped to get back their territory, and perhaps believed that the Indians would work such ruin to the republic as to make it easily conquered.

# CHAPTER

# FOURTEEN

---

## SUSPICIOUS BEHAVIOR

Under pretense of guarding against the coyotes, and preventing the cattle from straying, Father and I moved here and there in the vicinity of the house during the entire night, and I took note that one or the other of those teamsters was on the alert whenever we came near them, which fact caused Father's suspicions to increase rather than diminish, and we were thankful indeed when, at an early hour next morning, they took their departure.

Five or six weeks later, however, when we had fairly good proof that they were carrying muskets and, perhaps, ammunition to the Indians in order that an attack might be made on us settlers, Father regretted that he had not demanded to know what the fellows had in their carts.

When I asked him what he would have done if he had discovered that they were carrying weapons, he said most emphatically that, knowing the Indians on the border were in a state of unrest, he would have taken it upon himself to stop the fellows at the point of the rifle, and would have sent me to Fort Towson, even though I might have been forced to go alone, in order to learn what disposition should be made of them.

Mother said that it was fortunate for us that we

had not done any such wild thing, for if the fellows had resisted our attempts to search their carts, and resorted to weapons, then we might have come out second best.

# HUNTING WILD HOGS

Gyp and I thoroughly enjoyed ourselves hunting. He was not a dog trained for game, but he had so much good sound common sense that immediately after we had treed and killed our first wildcat, he entered into the sport as if he had been always accustomed to it.

Gyp was more like a comrade than like a brute. With the game as abundant as it then was on the West Fork of the Trinity, you can be assured that he and I, after the hardest of the work had been done, and when the sheep were not needing care, had some rare sport.

Having killed a cougar and scores upon scores of wolves, it was my desire to come across a drove of peccaries, as the wild hogs of Texas and Mexico are called. One day, when Zeba told me he had seen a drove of fifteen or twenty near the river, I set off without delay, Gyp at my heels, intending to bring back one or more that we might have a store of salt pork for the winter. Little did I dream what kind of animals I was going against!

We set off early in the morning, Gyp and I, and it seemed as if I had traveled at least seven miles before I came upon any signs of the wild hogs.

When I knew that a large number were close at hand, I began stalking them as I would a herd of deer. If I had known a little more about those vicious animals, I would have understood that at any show of enmity on my part I would bring them down upon me.

In fact, this was what I really did, although unwittingly. I supposed that such game, like others, would take to their heels at the first report of the rifle, and all I might succeed in getting would be at the first shot. Therefore I stole up toward the herd with the greatest caution, spending no less than an hour crawling through the mesquite bushes toward where I heard the little fellows grunting and squealing as they rooted among the decaying leaves for food.

No hunter could have asked for a better shot than I had. With a single ball I killed one of the peccaries, and wounded two others in such a manner that I had no doubt but that I could quickly bring them down. I began to reload the rifle, ordering Gyp to remain at my heels so he might not unduly alarm the drove. Hardly had I poured in the powder and rammed it home, when like a whirlwind all that drove of hogs charged through the mesquite bushes, and in the instant I was fleeing for my life.

Now it may seem odd that a fellow nearly thirteen years old should run away from a drove of hogs: but let me tell you that these were no ordinary animals, as my experience taught me. They were about half the size of a full-grown hog with very sharp snouts, wicked-looking tusks protruding from either side of the mouth, and long, slim legs, which told that they were fitted for a race.

# TREED BY PECCARIES

It is not to be supposed I gave particular heed to those characteristics while the peccaries were charging upon me, it was afterward, when I had an opportunity of seeing the dead animals at my leisure, that I noted their size and shape.

When they came at full speed toward me, with gnashing of teeth and grunts of anger, I said to myself that I would sooner be confronted by two cougars than by such a drove, and, realizing on the instant that there was little chance for me to escape by flight,

I sought refuge in a small pecan tree which stood near at hand.

It was well I moved quickly, for the foremost of the drove thrust at me viciously with his tusks, tearing off the bottom of my moccasin as I climbed up the tree and strove to take my rifle with me.

In an instant the hair on Gyp's back stood straight up, and he braced himself as if for a battle. Now despite the fact that I had had no acquaintance with peccaries, I understood at a single glance that he would have little show against their tusks, and therefore I shouted for him to go home.

The last of the hogs were charging down upon us when I repeated the order, and it was fortunate indeed for Gyp that he had learned to obey instantly any command I gave, although it was plain to be seen that he did not do so willingly.

# GYP'S OBEDIENCE

Despite my sharp words Gyp stood irresolute half a minute perhaps, and I thought he was about to spring upon the foe. I shouted yet more sternly, and the good dog wheeled about in a manner which told that he highly disapproved of my forcing him to turn his back upon an enemy, and trotted away.

The peccaries turned to follow him, whereupon I broke one of the stoutest branches within my reach and flung it among the drove as a challenge for them to turn their attention upon me and to give Gyp an opportunity to escape.

It seemed to me then that you need no more than a tone of defiance to provoke a row with peccaries, for when the branch hit the leader of the drove, he turned, with an angry grunt and snort, to face me. Following his example, the remainder of the drove saw me plainly as I leaned over in full view.

If, before we left Bolivar County, any one had told me I would flee for my life before a drove of hogs, and then allow myself to be held prisoner by them, I would have laughed heartily, and yet such was the case now.

The vicious little animals crowded against the trunk of the tree, leaping up as if hoping to get a hold upon me, and tearing off huge pieces of the bark in their efforts.

At first I was not inclined to believe the situation very serious, and said to myself that it was an opportunity to lay in as much fresh pork as we could use during the winter season. I therefore loaded my rifle leisurely and prepared to slaughter the entire drove.

# CHAPTER
# FIFTEEN

---

## MY CARELESSNESS

I fired two shots, bringing down a hog with each bullet. Then, through clumsiness or the difficulty of holding myself securely upon the small limb of the tree, the powder horn slipped from my fingers, and in an instant they had ground it to fragments.

It was useless to blame myself for such a blunder, and for the moment it did not seem to be very serious, since I expected that my enemies would soon go away after learning that it was impossible to get at me.

I had killed three outright, and wounded two so severely that they were lying on the ground; but of these the remainder of the drove appeared to take no notice whatsoever. Their only object was to get hold of me, and before ten minutes had passed I began to understand that I was not only regularly treed, but likely to remain a prisoner until they were forced to leave me in order to seek food.

They leaped, and grunted, and snarled, at the foot of the tree until, as time wore on, I became absolutely afraid that, growing exhausted, I might fall among them and be torn to pieces.

After a time I lost all desire to look at that ring of sharp tusks protruding from the red mouths which rose and swayed before me like some unearthly thing made up of many parts, and was actually grown so cowardly that I closed my eyes to shut out the sight.

# VICIOUS LITTLE ANIMALS

Hour after hour passed, yet those vicious little brutes at the foot of the tree seemed as excited as when they first saw me, and I made up my mind that I was in for many hours of this odd imprisonment, because it was not reasonable to suppose the hogs would soon grow so hungry as to leave me free.

But for the fact that Gyp was a dog who obeyed my every command, and had the good sense to under-stand that something serious had happened, I might have come to the end of my days there among the mesquite bushes, murdered by the peccaries I had counted on for pork.

Fortunately Father was about two miles down the river when he saw Gyp coming toward him apparently in great fright. At once he understood the situation to be extremely grave, else the dog would never have returned home without me. Seizing his rifle, for we on the banks of the Trinity took good care to go well armed even while working on the ranch, Father ordered Gyp to lead the way to where he had left me.

Half an hour before sunset he came so near that it was possible to hear the angry grunting of the peccaries, and understood in a twinkling what had happened.

## FATHER COMES TO THE RESCUE

His first care was to lift Gyp into a pecan twenty or thirty yards away from where I was roosting, and there the dog struggled to hold himself in the crotch of a limb while Father clambered up beside him.

All this while the hogs which were holding me prisoner gave no heed to the noise made by Father and Gyp, but continued their efforts to reach me by leaping up against the trunk of the tree until Father opened fire, shouting to me as he sent a bullet among them:—

"Are you safe, lad? Have you been hurt?"

"I am all right; but I have dropped my powder horn."

Then Father began firing as rapidly as the rifle could be reloaded. There were seventeen in the drove

I came upon; three I had killed and two I had wounded, leaving twelve very much alive and very active.

Father killed nine before the survivors decided that the time had come for them to beat a retreat, and when the last of the three trotted off, grunting and gnashing his teeth, I literally dropped from my perch in the pecan, as limp as though I had been ill for some time.

So far as getting a supply of pork was concerned, to say nothing of the saving of my life, it was well Father took a hand in the fight. We dressed the carcasses and hung up the meat on the branches of the trees to save it from being devoured by the wolves; after which, each of us carrying a peccary on his back, we set out for the long tramp home, I promising myself sorrowfully that never again would I go out hog hunting without taking due precautions against being worsted.

I shall spend no more time telling of the hunting which Gyp and I did, even though I am strongly tempted to do so; for we often had rare sport, both on the prairie and in the woods, in search of all kinds of game.

And there was game in great abundance, if we cared to go sufficiently far from home. One year after our arrival, however, there came to the banks of the Trinity four other families who staked out land and thus somewhat interfered with the freedom of our sport. It seemed to me, then, that the country was becoming too thickly settled, for I had to walk no more than five miles in order to reach the house of a man who had been our neighbor in Bolivar County.

# THE INCREASE IN MY FLOCK

In the spring of 1844, one year after our coming into the republic, Father decided to give me all his sheep as payment for the work I had performed on the ranch.

By this time our flock of seventy-two had increased to a hundred and fourteen, and we had good reason to hope that it would be doubled in numbers before another season had passed.

I then turned all my attention to herding sheep, driving them far out over the prairie where the grass was richest. There, day after day, Gyp and I remained, with no other covering than the sky above us, save when we spent our idle time putting up a temporary shelter here or there where we might be shielded from the too strong rays of the sun, or from the blasts of the norther. All the while my flock throve famously.

It seemed to me fortunate, so far as my own enterprise was concerned, that the new settlers on the banks of the Trinity had not brought with them any sheep, for they did not expect to raise such animals, having heard that the western part of the state was better adapted for the purpose.

Therefore I had no fear that the scab would come among my flock, because we were not in that section where strange sheep were likely to be driven from one point to another, and just so that I kept away from where the cattle were grazing, I had the entire northern portion of Texas for my own range, with no person to interfere.

# UNREST OF THE INDIANS

We had heard rumors of an uprising among the Indians when we came to Fort Towson, on our way from Bolivar County. Again, when the new settlers arrived, they told us that the Comanches were in a state of unrest.

We had still further reason to believe that some trouble might be expected, when those two Mexicans stopped at our ranch with cartloads of what were unquestionably rifles. Yet we gave little heed to the news. It seemed to us that we were so far in the wilderness, beyond reach of anyone else, that we would not be molested, whatever might take place, and all our efforts were bent toward improving the ranch and increasing our herds and flocks.

So far as I was concerned, I thought only of the sheep. I could not understand why the Indians should come where we were, because we had nothing to tempt them save our livestock.

We prospered exceedingly as time wore on, and lived contentedly, hearing little or nothing from the outer world. It was as if we were in a country by ourselves, for during the two years we had been on the Trinity we had had no visitors, except the two Mexicans and those settlers of whom I have spoken.

# CHAPTER
# SIXTEEN

## TEXAS JOINS THE UNION

Before coming into Texas to live we had heard it said that the citizens of the republic were making efforts to be annexed to the United States; but Father had given little heed to such talk, believing that the people of the States would hesitate lest difficulties with Mexico be brought about.

We knew nothing of what was going on outside our ranch, and were not counting on hearing important news. In the spring of 1845, while I was rejoicing over the wondrous increase in my flock, and Father was priding himself upon the fact that his land was growing each day more and more valuable, two mounted men drove up just at night-fall and asked for food and shelter. As we had not had any visitors for nearly two years, you cannot imagine how eager we were to grant their request, and how earnestly we strove to make them welcome.

In so doing we were well repaid, for then we learned that the Republic of Texas had ceased to exist. The visitors told us we were living in one of the states of the Union, for the act of annexation had been signed by President John Tyler on the first day of March in the year 1845, and a convention had been held later at Austin to ratify the resolution.

I had brought with me from Bolivar County a small American flag, but had not hoisted it because of being a citizen of the republic whose ensign contained but a single star.

Within five minutes after learning that Texas was really a part of the Union, I brought out the Stars and Stripes and fastened it to the topmost branches of the largest pecan tree in the motte. Then I saluted it with as many charges of powder as I could afford to spend, for you must know that on the Trinity at that time powder and ball were not only scarce but expensive.

My store of ammunition was nearly exhausted by such a celebration; but Father promised that very soon we would drive some of the cattle and a few of the sheep to Dallas, and

there sell them to get sufficient money to buy the sup-
plies which we were needing.

These visitors of ours had come to spy out the land
with an idea of making a settlement near our ranch,
and while it was pleasant to look forward to having
near neighbors, I was not pleased with the idea of being forced to take my flocks farther afield in order to
find fresh pasturage, as must happen in case many
people took up land in our vicinity.

For Mother's sake, however, I was pleased, because
she was filled with delight at the idea of having some-
one near with whom she could visit.

# WAR WITH MEXICO

With the coming of strangers, and the building of
new homes near us, we began to hear more of what
was being done in the outer world, and when Father
and Zeba went down to Dallas to sell a few cattle and
sheep, they brought back the surprising news that the
United States was at war with Mexico.

We were told that the younger men of Texas were
volunteering as soldiers, and that much blood might
be shed.

By this time I was fifteen years old, and it seemed
to me that it was my duty to leave home, and to aban-

don my plans of getting rich through sheep raising, in order to do what I could in defense of the state of which I claimed to be a citizen.

Father soon gave me to understand, however, that I was not yet old enough to take up arms. He insisted that duty called me to remain where I was, and that we were doing our duty by the state so long as we remained on the ranch raising livestock, for if war was continued any length of time, cattle and sheep would be required in order to supply the army with food.

I therefore gave up all thoughts of enlisting. Perhaps I was the more willing to do this because of the sorrow that I should feel if forced to leave my flock, which now numbered nearly five hundred. But whenever John or Zeba was at liberty to herd my flock, I frequently walked many miles in order to learn what was going on in the war.

# SELLING WOOL

I was the one who brought to our ranch the news that the Mexicans had bombarded Fort Brown, May 4, 1846,

when Major Brown was killed; also word from Dallas of the battle of Palo Alto. Then we heard from Mon-

terey, and but for the fact that I had three years' shearing of wool to sell, I believe I might have enlisted after
all.

It was necessary, however, that I sell this wool at a
time when the prices were high, and during the two
months which followed the battle of Monterey I spent
all my time freighting the fleeces from the ranch to

Dallas, using one of the big wagons with eight mules,
and taking Zeba with me as assistant.

When I had in my pocket the money which had
been paid for the wool, it seemed as if I might really
call myself a ranchman. I was so proud of my success
that I almost lost sight of the fact that other young
fellows, most likely some of them no older than I,

were putting on the uniforms of enlisted men, and taking their places in the ranks to defend the state in which were their homes.

Once we heard that the Comanches were on the warpath, and there were times when it seemed certain we might be attacked at any moment. Then Father put Bar-O Ranch in a state of defense. He brought from Dallas a good supply of weapons, and we fitted to the windows of our house heavy shutters in which were loopholes, but in the end we had no need of them.

# PEACE ON THE TRINITY

The Lord was good to us settlers on the Trinity. It seemed at times almost as if it was a crime for us to prosper so wondrously well, while in other parts of the state the settlers were struggling. Indeed, I was very nearly ashamed because no harm came to us on the Trinity, because our worldly goods were increasing day by day, and because Bar-O Ranch was rapidly becoming one of the best in the state.

But for the fact that many others have told the story of how Texas won her independence, how she flourished or decayed as a free republic during ten years, and how she was finally annexed to the United States, I would be glad to tell more of these things to you. They could not fail to be entertaining as well as instructive, for they show how a people with a true purpose before them overcame the many obstacles which confronted them and finally made Texas what she is to-day, one of the brightest stars in the blue field of Old Glory.

# MY DREAM FULFILLED

I may not have done all I might toward the settlement of this grand state, but the dream which was mine in Bolivar County has at last been fulfilled. The flock which numbered twelve when I left the old home has increased to more than five thousand, and my sale of wool each year amounts to as much as that of any other ranchman within two hundred miles of us. Furthermore, in addition to my sheep, I claim a full interest with Father in Bar-O Ranch, which is in itself no mean property, and am duly thankful for all the good things of this life which have come to me.

Yet there is in my heart at this moment, and ever will be, a keen regret, that I entirely forgot one admonition from the Bible which has in these past years stood out so boldly in my mind. How much better is it to get wisdom than gold! And to get understanding is rather to be chosen than silver.

It is true there were no opportunities for me when we first settled on the banks of the Trinity, but if I had struggled half as hard to get wisdom as I have struggled to hold my flocks prosperous, then I could now look back with real pride upon what I have accomplished.

If I had done this, there would now be no happier person in this great state than Philip of Texas.